Table Of Contents

Chapter 1: Understanding Branding in the Trade Industry — 2

Chapter 2: Developing Your Brand Identity — 9

Chapter 3: Marketing Strategies for Trade Business Owners — 15

Chapter 4: Referral Marketing Techniques — 22

Chapter 5: Social Media and Online Presence — 29

Chapter 6: Networking and Building Relationships — 36

Chapter 7: Measuring Your Brand Success — 43

Chapter 8: Future Trends in Trade Branding — 49

Chapter 9: Case Studies of Successful Trade Brands — 57

Chapter 10: Building a Sustainable Brand — 64

01

Chapter 1: Understanding Branding in the Trade Industry

The Importance of Branding for Trade Professionals

Branding holds significant importance for trade professionals, serving as a foundation for establishing credibility and trust in a competitive marketplace. In an industry often characterized by a myriad of choices, a strong brand can differentiate a business from its competitors. Trade business owners must recognize that effective branding goes beyond a logo or color scheme; it encompasses the entire customer experience, from initial contact through to post-service follow-up. A well-defined brand identity communicates not only what the business does but also its values, mission, and commitment to quality, which are crucial in fostering customer loyalty.

The role of branding in marketing for trade businesses cannot be overstated. It creates a recognizable identity that resonates with target audiences. A consistent brand message across various marketing channels—such as social media, websites, and print materials—reinforces the business's presence and enhances recall among potential clients. Trade professionals should invest time and resources into developing a cohesive branding strategy that aligns with their market positioning. This includes creating compelling narratives that showcase their expertise and the unique benefits they offer, which can be pivotal in attracting and retaining customers.

Moreover, branding is pivotal in referral marketing techniques, which are essential for trade businesses. Satisfied customers are more likely to recommend a brand that they identify with and trust. A strong brand not only facilitates positive word-of-mouth but also encourages repeat business, as clients feel a sense of loyalty to a brand they recognize and appreciate. Trade professionals can leverage their branding efforts to create memorable experiences that motivate customers to share their positive experiences with others, ultimately expanding their client base through referrals.

Additionally, a strong brand identity can enhance a trade professional's ability to charge premium prices for their services. When customers perceive a brand as reputable and high-quality, they are often willing to pay more. This perception stems from effective branding that conveys professionalism, reliability, and value. Trade business owners should focus on building a brand that communicates quality and expertise, as this can significantly influence pricing strategies and profitability. Investing in branding can lead to long-term financial benefits, making it a crucial aspect of business strategy.

Finally, branding provides trade professionals with an opportunity to connect with their target audience on a deeper level. By aligning their brand with the values and aspirations of their customers, trade business owners can foster loyalty and advocacy. This emotional connection is essential, as it transforms customers into brand champions who actively promote the business within their networks. By understanding the importance of branding and its role in marketing, referrals, and customer loyalty, trade professionals can create a robust branding strategy that drives sustainable growth and success in their businesses.

Key Elements of a Strong Brand

A strong brand is essential for trade business owners looking to differentiate themselves in a competitive marketplace. Key elements of a strong brand include a clear brand identity, consistent messaging, emotional connection, a unique value proposition, and a customer-centric approach. Each of these elements plays a crucial role in establishing a brand that resonates with both existing and potential customers, ultimately driving loyalty and referrals.

The foundation of any strong brand is its identity, which encompasses the brand name, logo, colors, and overall aesthetic. This identity should reflect the values and mission of the business while appealing to the target audience. For trade professionals, a well-crafted identity can convey expertise, reliability, and professionalism. It is paramount that the visual elements are consistently applied across all platforms, from business cards to websites, ensuring that customers recognize and remember the brand at every touchpoint.

Consistent messaging is another critical component of a strong brand. This involves developing a clear voice and tone that aligns with the brand identity and resonates with the target audience. Trade business owners should ensure that their messaging reflects their unique expertise and the specific benefits of their services. Consistency across marketing materials, social media, and customer interactions helps build trust and reinforces the brand in the minds of consumers.

Creating an emotional connection with customers can significantly enhance brand loyalty. Trade professionals can do this by sharing stories that highlight their passion for their work, the challenges they solve, and the positive impact they have on clients. By showcasing real-life examples and testimonials, businesses can foster a sense of community and belonging, making customers feel valued and understood. This connection not only encourages repeat business but also facilitates word-of-mouth referrals, which are vital in the trade industry.

A unique value proposition distinguishes a brand from its competitors and explains why customers should choose one service over another. For trade professionals, identifying what sets their business apart—whether it's superior craftsmanship, exceptional customer service, or innovative solutions—is essential. This proposition should be clearly communicated in all marketing efforts, making it easy for potential customers to understand the benefits of choosing that particular brand. Lastly, adopting a customer-centric approach, where feedback is actively sought and integrated into service offerings, ensures that the brand evolves with its audience, enhancing relevance and loyalty over time.

Common Branding Mistakes in Trade Businesses

Trade business owners often overlook crucial aspects of branding that can significantly impact their success. One common mistake is failing to define a clear brand identity. Many businesses in the trade sector operate under generic names and logos that do not convey their unique offerings or values. Without a distinct identity, these businesses struggle to differentiate themselves in a crowded market, leading to missed opportunities for recognition and customer loyalty. A well-defined brand identity not only sets a business apart but also helps potential customers understand what the company stands for and what they can expect.

Another frequent error is neglecting to understand the target audience. Trade professionals often assume that their services will appeal to everyone, which can dilute their marketing efforts. By not identifying and focusing on a specific audience, businesses may invest resources in marketing channels that do not yield results. Understanding the demographics, preferences, and pain points of the target market enables trade businesses to tailor their messaging and promotional strategies, leading to more effective engagement and conversion rates.

Inconsistent branding across various platforms is a significant pitfall for many trade businesses. When branding elements such as logos, color schemes, and messaging differ from one platform to another, it creates confusion among potential customers and undermines brand credibility. Consistency fosters trust and recognition, essential elements for building a strong brand. Trade professionals should ensure that their branding is uniform across all channels, including websites, social media, and marketing materials, to create a cohesive and professional image.

Failing to leverage customer testimonials and referrals is another common mistake. Trade businesses often underestimate the power of word-of-mouth marketing. Satisfied customers can become powerful brand advocates, but if businesses do not actively seek and showcase testimonials, they miss out on valuable social proof. Encouraging happy clients to share their experiences and incorporating those testimonials into marketing efforts can enhance credibility and attract new customers. Additionally, implementing a referral program can incentivize existing clients to recommend services to their networks, further expanding brand reach.

Lastly, trade business owners frequently neglect the importance of ongoing brand evaluation and adaptation. The market landscape is constantly evolving, and what worked yesterday may not resonate today. Failing to assess brand performance and customer feedback can lead to stagnation. Trade professionals should regularly review their branding strategies, gather insights from their audience, and be willing to make adjustments as needed. This proactive approach not only keeps a brand relevant but also demonstrates a commitment to meeting customer needs, ultimately driving growth and success in the competitive trade industry.

02

Chapter 2: Developing Your Brand Identity

Defining Your Brand Values

Defining your brand values is a critical step in establishing a strong identity for your trade business. Brand values represent the core principles that guide your company's culture, decision-making, and interactions with customers. These values resonate beyond the products or services you offer; they reflect your company's beliefs and commitments. For trade business owners, articulating these values can enhance customer loyalty, differentiate your business from competitors, and create a cohesive company culture that aligns with your mission.

To begin defining your brand values, consider what is most important to you as a business owner. Reflect on your personal values and how they translate into your business philosophy. Think about the qualities that you want your business to embody, such as integrity, quality, or innovation. Engage your team in discussions about what they believe the company stands for and how they would like to be perceived by clients. This collaborative approach not only fosters a sense of ownership among employees but also helps in crafting values that truly represent the heart of your business.

Once you have a preliminary list of values, it is essential to refine and prioritize them. Select a handful of core values that encapsulate your business's identity and mission. These should be values that you are willing to uphold consistently, even in challenging situations. For trade businesses, it can be beneficial to focus on values that resonate with your target audience, such as customer service excellence or sustainability. By clearly defining and articulating these core values, you create a framework that guides your decision-making and branding strategies.

Communicating your brand values effectively is crucial for making them resonate with your audience. Incorporate these values into your marketing materials, website, and social media presence. Share stories that illustrate how your business embodies these values in action, whether through customer testimonials, case studies, or behind-the-scenes glimpses of your operations. Consistent messaging reinforces your commitment to these values and helps customers connect with your brand on a deeper level, facilitating trust and loyalty.

Lastly, it is important to revisit and reassess your brand values periodically. As your trade business evolves, so too may your values and the expectations of your customers. Stay attuned to industry trends and customer feedback to ensure that your values remain relevant and aligned with your business goals. By continuously reflecting on and adapting your brand values, you can maintain a strong, authentic identity that resonates with your audience and positions your trade business for long-term success.

Crafting Your Brand Story

Crafting a compelling brand story is essential for trade business owners looking to distinguish themselves in a competitive market. A well-articulated brand story not only captures the essence of your business but also resonates with your audience on a personal level. This narrative should encapsulate your values, mission, and the unique journey that led you to establish your trade business. By weaving these elements together, you create a powerful narrative that can engage potential customers and foster loyalty among existing ones.

To begin crafting your brand story, start by reflecting on your origins. Consider the motivations that drove you to enter the trade. Was it a family tradition, a passion for craftsmanship, or a desire to solve a specific problem in your community? Sharing these foundational elements helps humanize your brand and makes it relatable. Furthermore, incorporating personal anecdotes and experiences can add depth to your story, allowing your audience to connect with you on a more emotional level.

Next, focus on the core values that guide your business. These values should reflect what your trade business stands for and how you wish to be perceived in the marketplace. Are you committed to sustainability, exceptional customer service, or innovation? Clearly articulating these principles not only enhances your brand identity but also signals to your customers what they can expect when they engage with your business. Consistency in delivering on these values will reinforce your brand story and build trust over time.

Additionally, highlight the challenges you have faced and overcome throughout your journey. Every business encounters obstacles, and sharing these experiences can demonstrate resilience and determination. By narrating how you navigated difficulties, you can illustrate your problem-solving abilities and dedication to your craft. This aspect of your story can be particularly appealing to potential customers, as they often seek businesses that exhibit grit and reliability.

Finally, ensure that your brand story evolves as your business grows. As you gain new experiences, expand your services, or enter new markets, your narrative should adapt to reflect these changes. Regularly revisiting and refining your brand story can keep it relevant and engaging. Incorporating customer testimonials or success stories can also enrich your narrative, showcasing the impact your trade business has had on others. A dynamic brand story not only engages your audience but also positions your trade business as a trusted leader in your field.

Designing Your Visual Identity

Designing your visual identity is a crucial step for trade business owners looking to establish a strong brand presence in a competitive market. Your visual identity encompasses the elements that communicate your brand's personality, values, and professionalism. This includes your logo, color palette, typography, and any imagery you utilize in your marketing materials. A well-thought-out visual identity not only helps differentiate your business from competitors but also creates a cohesive experience for your customers, enhancing brand recognition and loyalty.

The logo is often the first interaction potential clients have with your brand, making it vital to invest time and resources into its design. A strong logo should be simple, memorable, and relevant to your trade. Consider elements that reflect your specific niche, whether it's construction, plumbing, or electrical services. Engaging with a graphic designer who understands your industry can provide insights into creating a logo that resonates with your target audience while conveying professionalism and trustworthiness.

Color plays a significant role in how your brand is perceived. Different colors evoke different emotions and associations, and selecting a color palette that aligns with your brand values is essential. For example, blue often represents reliability and trust, while green can signify growth and sustainability. When choosing your colors, consider how they will appear across various platforms, from your website to your business cards and work vehicles. A consistent color scheme helps to reinforce your brand identity and makes your materials instantly recognizable.

Typography is another critical component of your visual identity. The fonts you choose should reflect your brand's personality and be legible across all mediums. A construction business may opt for bold, strong typefaces, while a plumbing service might choose clean and straightforward fonts to convey clarity and simplicity. Consistency in typography across your marketing materials will help solidify your brand image and ensure that your messaging is coherent and professional.

Imagery is the final piece of the visual identity puzzle. The images you select for your website, social media, and promotional materials should not only align with your brand but also resonate with your target audience. High-quality images that showcase your work, your team, or satisfied customers can enhance your credibility and appeal. Additionally, incorporating your brand colors and style into these images can further reinforce your visual identity. By thoughtfully designing your visual identity, you create a powerful tool to attract and retain customers, ultimately supporting your business's growth and success.

03

Chapter 3: Marketing Strategies for Trade Business Owners

Identifying Your Target Audience

Identifying your target audience is a crucial step in developing an effective branding strategy for your trade business. Understanding who your ideal customers are allows you to tailor your marketing efforts, ensuring that your messaging resonates with them. Start by analyzing the demographics of your existing client base. Consider factors such as age, gender, income level, location, and occupation. This data can provide insights into who is most likely to benefit from your services and help you focus your marketing efforts on those segments.

Next, delve into psychographics to gain a deeper understanding of your target audience's motivations, values, and interests. Psychographics go beyond basic demographics and examine the lifestyle choices and attitudes of your potential customers. For trade business owners, this means understanding what drives your audience's purchasing decisions, such as quality, price, or brand reputation.

Conduct surveys or interviews with past clients to gather qualitative data about their preferences and pain points, which can inform your branding and marketing strategies.

Competitor analysis is another effective method for identifying your target audience. By examining the customer base of your competitors, you can uncover gaps in the market and identify potential audiences that you may not have previously considered. Look at their marketing materials, online presence, and customer reviews to determine who they are targeting and how effectively they are reaching those customers. This analysis can help you differentiate your brand and identify unique selling propositions that appeal to your target audience.

Once you have a clear understanding of your target audience, create customer personas to represent different segments of your market. These personas should encapsulate the demographics, psychographics, and pain points of your ideal customers. For trade business owners, developing detailed customer personas can guide your marketing strategies, ensuring that your messaging is relevant and compelling. Each persona can inform various aspects of your branding, from the tone of your communication to the channels you choose for outreach.

Finally, continuously reassess and adjust your understanding of your target audience as your business evolves. Market trends, economic conditions, and customer preferences can shift over time, making it essential to stay attuned to these changes. Regularly solicit feedback from your customers and monitor the effectiveness of your marketing campaigns to ensure that you remain aligned with your audience's needs. By maintaining a dynamic understanding of your target audience, you can adapt your branding efforts to foster loyalty and drive growth in your trade business.

Building an Effective Marketing Plan

Building an effective marketing plan is essential for trade business owners aiming to establish a strong brand presence and drive consistent growth. The first step in creating a marketing plan is to define your target audience clearly. Understanding who your ideal customers are, their demographics, preferences, and pain points enables you to tailor your marketing efforts effectively. Conducting market research and gathering insights about your audience will help you create a more focused approach, ensuring that your marketing messages resonate with potential clients.

Once you have a clear understanding of your audience, the next step is to set specific, measurable goals. These goals should align with your overall business objectives and can include increasing brand awareness, generating leads, or boosting sales. Utilizing the SMART criteria—Specific, Measurable, Achievable, Relevant, Time-bound—will help you create actionable goals that can be tracked over time. This clarity will not only guide your marketing efforts but also provide benchmarks to measure success and make necessary adjustments.

Developing a unique value proposition is crucial in differentiating your trade business from competitors. Your value proposition should communicate what sets your services apart and why customers should choose you over others. This message should be consistent across all marketing channels, from your website to social media and print materials. A well-articulated value proposition not only enhances your branding but also builds credibility and trust with potential clients, making them more likely to engage with your business.

To effectively reach your target audience, you must choose the right marketing channels. Depending on your niche and audience preferences, this could include digital marketing strategies such as social media, email marketing, or search engine optimization, as well as traditional methods like print advertising or networking events. A multi-channel approach often yields the best results, allowing you to connect with your audience in various ways. Regularly evaluating the performance of each channel will enable you to optimize your strategy over time.

Lastly, referral marketing is a powerful tool for trade businesses to leverage. Encouraging satisfied customers to refer your services to others can significantly enhance your client base without substantial marketing spend. Implementing a referral program that incentivizes customers for referrals can motivate them to spread the word about your business. Combining this with testimonials and case studies can further build trust and credibility, driving more leads and fostering long-term relationships with clients. By incorporating these elements into your marketing plan, trade business owners can create a robust strategy that not only promotes their brand but also ensures sustainable growth.

Utilizing Digital Marketing Tools

Digital marketing tools have transformed the landscape for trade business owners, offering innovative ways to enhance visibility, engage with clients, and streamline operations. By leveraging these tools, trade professionals can create a robust online presence that reflects their brand identity while reaching a wider audience. Platforms such as social media, email marketing, and content management systems provide the necessary infrastructure to connect with potential customers and foster relationships that lead to referrals and repeat business.

Social media platforms like Facebook, Instagram, and LinkedIn are vital for trade businesses to showcase their work and interact with clients. These platforms allow trade professionals to post images of completed projects, share testimonials, and engage in conversations with their audience. By actively participating in these communities, business owners can build trust and credibility, essential components of a strong brand identity. Furthermore, targeted advertising on these platforms enables trade professionals to reach specific demographics, ensuring their marketing efforts are both efficient and effective.

Email marketing remains a powerful tool for maintaining communication with clients and prospects. Trade business owners can utilize email campaigns to share industry insights, project updates, and promotional offers, keeping their audience informed and engaged. By segmenting their email lists, trade professionals can tailor their messages to specific groups, enhancing the relevance of their communication. This personalized approach can significantly improve response rates and foster a sense of loyalty among customers, ultimately driving referrals and repeat business.

Content marketing is another crucial aspect of utilizing digital tools for branding and identity development. By creating valuable content, such as blogs, videos, and how-to guides, trade professionals can establish themselves as industry experts. This not only enhances their brand image but also attracts potential clients searching for solutions to their problems. High-quality content can improve search engine rankings, making it easier for prospective customers to find trade businesses online. Additionally, incorporating SEO best practices into content creation helps ensure that the brand is visible in relevant search results, driving organic traffic.

Finally, analytics and tracking tools provide trade business owners with valuable insights into their marketing efforts. By monitoring website traffic, social media engagement, and email open rates, professionals can assess the effectiveness of their strategies and make data-driven decisions. Understanding which tactics resonate with their audience allows trade owners to optimize their marketing campaigns, allocate resources more efficiently, and ultimately enhance their brand's impact. By embracing these digital marketing tools, trade professionals can create a comprehensive branding strategy that not only promotes their services but also fosters long-term relationships with their clients.

04

Chapter 4: Referral Marketing Techniques

The Power of Word-of-Mouth

In the realm of trade businesses, word-of-mouth marketing stands out as one of the most influential and cost-effective promotional tools available. This organic form of communication occurs when satisfied customers share their positive experiences with others, creating a ripple effect that can significantly enhance brand visibility and credibility. For trade professionals, harnessing the power of word-of-mouth can lead to a steady stream of referrals, ultimately driving growth and establishing a strong reputation within the community.

One of the key advantages of word-of-mouth marketing is its authenticity. Potential customers are often more inclined to trust recommendations from friends, family, or colleagues than traditional advertising. This trust is particularly important in the trade sector, where the quality of work and reliability can vary significantly. By delivering exceptional service and fostering strong relationships with clients, trade business owners can encourage satisfied customers to become advocates for their brand, promoting their services to others without any prompting.

To maximize the effectiveness of word-of-mouth marketing, trade professionals should focus on creating memorable customer experiences. This involves not only delivering high-quality work but also providing excellent customer service throughout the entire process. Engaging with clients, addressing their concerns, and following up after the completion of a project can leave a lasting impression. Additionally, trade business owners can implement strategies such as requesting feedback and encouraging clients to leave reviews, helping to solidify their reputation as trustworthy providers in their niche.

Referral programs can also serve as a powerful complement to word-of-mouth marketing. By incentivizing existing customers to refer new clients, trade professionals can amplify their reach and deepen the impact of their satisfied clients' recommendations. Offering discounts, freebies, or other rewards for successful referrals not only motivates current customers to spread the word but also fosters loyalty and encourages repeated business. Trade business owners should carefully design these programs to ensure they align with their brand values and resonate with their target audience.

Finally, trade business owners should leverage digital platforms to enhance their word-of-mouth marketing efforts. Social media, online review sites, and community forums provide avenues for clients to share their experiences with a broader audience. By actively engaging with clients on these platforms and showcasing positive testimonials, trade professionals can further amplify their brand message. Creating shareable content that encourages customers to express their satisfaction online can lead to increased visibility and a stronger brand presence in the competitive trade market.

Creating a Referral Program

Creating a referral program is a strategic approach that trade business owners can implement to leverage their existing customer base for new client acquisition. A well-crafted referral program not only enhances customer loyalty but also establishes a network of advocates who can promote your services through word-of-mouth. This method is particularly effective in the trade industry, where personal recommendations carry significant weight in decision-making processes. By incentivizing referrals, you can turn satisfied customers into active promoters of your brand.

The first step in creating a successful referral program is to clearly define your objectives. Determine what you hope to achieve through the program, whether it's increasing your customer base, enhancing brand awareness, or boosting sales revenue. Establish specific, measurable goals that will allow you to assess the effectiveness of your program over time. Understanding your target audience and the key motivations that drive them to refer others is crucial at this stage. This insight will help you tailor your program to align with their preferences and behaviors.

Next, design an attractive incentive structure that motivates customers to participate in your referral program. Consider various rewards, such as discounts on future services, gift cards, or exclusive offers. The key is to ensure that the incentives are appealing enough to encourage referrals while remaining sustainable for your business. Additionally, consider implementing tiered rewards that increase with the number of successful referrals, creating a sense of competition and continued engagement. This structure not only rewards individual customers but also fosters a community spirit among your clientele.

Once your program is designed, it's essential to promote it effectively. Utilize multiple channels to inform your customers about the referral program, including email newsletters, social media, and direct communication during service interactions. Make the process of referring others as seamless as possible; provide customers with easy-to-use referral links, promotional materials, or even referral cards they can share with friends and family. The easier you make it for customers to refer others, the more likely they are to take action.

Finally, monitor and evaluate the performance of your referral program regularly. Track key metrics such as the number of referrals generated, the conversion rate of those referrals, and the overall impact on your revenue. Solicit feedback from participants to identify areas for improvement and to understand their experiences with the program. By continuously refining your approach based on real-world results and customer input, you can enhance the effectiveness of your referral program and ensure it remains a valuable component of your marketing strategy.

Leveraging Customer Testimonials

Leveraging customer testimonials is a powerful strategy for trade business owners looking to enhance their branding and marketing efforts. In an industry where trust and reliability are paramount, showcasing the positive experiences of satisfied customers can significantly influence potential clients' decisions. Testimonials serve as social proof, demonstrating that your services not only meet but exceed customer expectations. By strategically incorporating testimonials into your marketing materials and online presence, you can build credibility and foster trust among prospective clients.

To effectively leverage customer testimonials, it is essential to gather them systematically. Encourage satisfied clients to share their feedback after completing a project. This can be done through follow-up emails, feedback forms, or even in-person conversations. Providing simple templates or guiding questions can help customers articulate their experiences more clearly, resulting in more impactful testimonials. Additionally, consider offering incentives for customers who participate in your testimonial program, such as discounts on future services or entry into a prize drawing. This not only motivates clients to provide feedback but also fosters a stronger relationship between your business and your customers.

Once you have collected testimonials, the next step is to showcase them prominently in your marketing efforts. Incorporate compelling quotes from customers into your website, brochures, and social media posts. Visual elements, such as photos of the completed projects alongside customer testimonials, can further enhance their impact. Video testimonials are particularly effective, as they allow potential clients to see and hear real customers discuss their positive experiences with your business. By utilizing a variety of formats, you can engage different audience preferences and increase the likelihood of resonating with potential clients.

Another critical aspect of leveraging customer testimonials is ensuring they are authentic and relatable. Prospective clients are more likely to connect with testimonials from individuals who share similar backgrounds or needs. When selecting testimonials to feature, aim for a diverse range of clients that reflect the various demographics of your target audience. This diversity can help potential clients envision themselves working with your business, thereby increasing the likelihood of conversion. Additionally, don't hesitate to include constructive feedback alongside positive testimonials. Addressing any minor criticisms can demonstrate your commitment to continuous improvement and customer satisfaction.

Finally, regularly updating your testimonials is essential to maintain their relevance and effectiveness. As your business evolves, so too will your customer base and the services you offer. Periodically review your testimonials to ensure they reflect your current capabilities and the latest customer experiences. Encourage ongoing feedback and engagement from your clients, emphasizing that their opinions are valued and integral to your business's growth. By consistently leveraging customer testimonials, trade business owners can not only enhance their branding and marketing strategies but also cultivate a loyal customer base built on trust and satisfaction.

05

Chapter 5: Social Media and Online Presence

Choosing the Right Platforms

Choosing the right platforms for your trade business is crucial for effectively reaching your target audience and building a strong brand presence. With numerous options available, it is essential to assess which platforms align best with your business goals and your audience's preferences. Understanding your audience's behavior will guide you in selecting the most effective channels for communication and engagement. This can include social media platforms, industry-specific forums, and local community pages that resonate with your customer base.

Social media has become a powerful tool for trade businesses to showcase their work, share customer testimonials, and connect with potential clients. Platforms like Facebook, Instagram, and LinkedIn offer unique advantages. Facebook is ideal for community engagement and sharing project updates, while Instagram allows for visual storytelling through images and videos of your work. LinkedIn, on the other hand, is beneficial for networking with other professionals and establishing your business credibility. Analyzing where your audience spends their time online will help you focus your efforts on the most effective social channels.

In addition to social media, consider industry-specific platforms and forums that cater to your niche. Websites and online communities that focus on trade-related topics can provide valuable opportunities for networking and collaboration. Participating in discussions, sharing expertise, and offering solutions to common problems can enhance your visibility and position you as an authority in your field. These platforms often attract an audience that is already interested in trade services, increasing the likelihood of generating quality leads.

Email marketing remains a powerful platform for trade business owners looking to maintain direct communication with their clients. Developing a mailing list allows you to share updates, promotions, and valuable content that keeps your audience engaged. Crafting informative newsletters can help reinforce your brand identity while providing insights into your services and industry trends. By segmenting your email lists based on customer preferences and behaviors, you can tailor your messaging to meet the specific needs of different audience segments, improving engagement and conversion rates.

Finally, do not overlook the importance of local platforms and directories. Trade businesses often thrive on local clientele, making it essential to establish a presence on platforms such as Google My Business, Yelp, and local trade associations. These platforms can enhance your visibility in local searches and provide potential customers with easy access to your contact information, service details, and customer reviews. By strategically selecting the right platforms, you can create a cohesive branding strategy that effectively reaches and resonates with your target audience, ultimately driving growth for your trade business.

Creating Engaging Content

Creating engaging content is essential for trade business owners who seek to enhance their branding and attract potential clients. Engaging content goes beyond mere promotion; it educates, informs, and resonates with the audience. For trade professionals, this means showcasing expertise in a way that is accessible and meaningful to clients. By focusing on the unique challenges and needs within the trade industry, business owners can craft narratives that speak directly to their target demographic, establishing trust and credibility.

One effective method for creating engaging content is to leverage storytelling. Trade professionals possess a wealth of experiences and knowledge that can be transformed into compelling narratives. By sharing real-life case studies or customer success stories, business owners can illustrate their problem-solving capabilities and the value they bring to clients. This approach not only captivates the audience but also demonstrates authenticity and relatability, which are crucial for building a strong brand identity in the trade sector.

Incorporating visual elements into content can significantly enhance engagement. The trade industry often involves complex processes and tangible results that can be better understood through visuals. Infographics, videos, and photographs of completed projects can provide insight into the quality of work and craftsmanship. These visuals not only attract attention but also serve as a powerful tool for explaining services and showcasing expertise. A well-crafted visual strategy can elevate content, making it more shareable and appealing across various platforms.

Consistency is key when it comes to content creation. Trade business owners should establish a content calendar that aligns with their branding goals and audience interests. This schedule should include a mix of blog posts, social media updates, newsletters, and other formats to maintain a steady flow of information. Consistent messaging reinforces brand identity and keeps the audience engaged over time. Additionally, regularly updating content ensures that trade professionals remain relevant and visible in a competitive market.

Finally, encouraging interaction can significantly boost engagement levels. Trade business owners should invite feedback and questions from their audience, fostering a two-way communication channel. This can be achieved through comment sections, social media platforms, or even through direct surveys. By actively engaging with clients and prospects, trade professionals can gain valuable insights into their audience's needs and preferences. This feedback can inform future content strategies and help businesses adapt to changing market dynamics, ultimately strengthening their brand presence and customer relationships.

Managing Online Reputation

Managing online reputation is crucial for trade business owners looking to establish and maintain a positive brand image. In today's digital landscape, consumers increasingly rely on online reviews, social media interactions, and search engine results to form perceptions about businesses. Consequently, it is essential for trade professionals to actively monitor their online presence and engage with their audience. A proactive approach to managing online reputation not only helps to mitigate negative feedback but also enhances the overall branding strategy.

To effectively manage online reputation, trade business owners should begin by conducting regular audits of their online presence. This includes monitoring review sites, social media platforms, and search engine results. By understanding what customers are saying about their business, owners can identify areas for improvement and address any negative comments promptly. Tools like Google Alerts and social media monitoring software can assist in tracking mentions of the business across various platforms. By staying informed, trade professionals can respond to customer feedback in real-time, demonstrating their commitment to customer satisfaction.

Engaging with customers is another vital component of managing online reputation. Trade business owners should encourage satisfied clients to leave positive reviews and testimonials, which can significantly influence potential customers. By actively asking for feedback, businesses can create a culture of appreciation that fosters loyalty and encourages referrals. Additionally, responding to reviews—both positive and negative—shows that the business values customer input and is willing to improve based on that feedback. This two-way communication helps build trust and enhances the overall brand image.

Incorporating a consistent branding strategy across all online platforms can further strengthen a trade business's reputation. This includes maintaining a professional website, using consistent branding elements such as logos and color schemes, and delivering a cohesive message across social media channels. A strong and recognizable brand identity not only helps differentiate a trade professional from competitors but also instills confidence in potential customers. Consistency in branding reinforces professionalism and reliability, contributing positively to the business's online reputation.

Finally, trade business owners should be prepared to address crises swiftly and effectively. In the event of negative publicity or an unfavorable review, it's essential to respond calmly and constructively. Acknowledging the issue, providing a solution, and taking the conversation offline can help mitigate the situation. Properly managing these challenging scenarios can turn a negative experience into an opportunity for growth, demonstrating to potential customers that the business is committed to high standards of service. By taking control of their online reputation, trade professionals can enhance their branding efforts and drive long-term success.

06

Chapter 6: Networking and Building Relationships

The Role of Networking in Trade Industries

Networking plays a crucial role in trade industries, serving as a foundational element for business development and growth. For trade business owners, establishing and nurturing professional relationships can lead to new opportunities, collaborations, and insights that are vital in a competitive marketplace. Networking is not just about exchanging business cards; it involves building meaningful connections that can enhance brand visibility and credibility within the industry.

In the realm of marketing for trade business owners, networking offers a platform to showcase expertise and share knowledge. Engaging with other professionals at industry events, trade shows, or local business gatherings allows owners to position themselves as thought leaders. This visibility is essential for attracting clients who seek trusted professionals. Additionally, networking can provide access to industry trends and best practices, enabling business owners to adapt their marketing strategies effectively to meet the evolving needs of their target audience.

Branding and identity development is another area significantly impacted by networking. Trade professionals can leverage their connections to enhance their brand's reputation and recognition. Through collaborative projects or partnerships, businesses can co-brand and reach wider audiences. A strong network also facilitates the sharing of testimonials and endorsements, which are invaluable for building trust and authority in the trade sector. The relationships cultivated through networking can serve as a powerful tool for reinforcing brand identity and establishing a distinctive market presence.

Referral marketing techniques are closely tied to effective networking. Business owners who actively participate in their professional communities often find that referrals flow naturally from these interactions. When trade professionals build genuine relationships, they create a network of advocates who are willing to recommend their services. This organic form of marketing is not only cost-effective but also tends to yield high-quality leads, as referrals come with an inherent level of trust. Encouraging referrals through networking can significantly boost a trade business's client base and overall revenue.

Ultimately, the role of networking in trade industries cannot be overstated. It is an essential strategy for marketing, branding, and generating referrals. Trade business owners who invest time and effort in building their networks are likely to experience greater opportunities for collaboration and growth. By prioritizing networking, they can enhance their professional presence, foster meaningful relationships, and ultimately drive the success of their businesses in a competitive landscape.

Effective Networking Strategies

Networking is a crucial component for trade business owners seeking to enhance their brand visibility and establish strong industry connections. Building a robust professional network allows trade professionals to share knowledge, gain referrals, and discover new business opportunities. One effective strategy for networking is to participate in industry-specific events such as trade shows, conferences, and workshops. These gatherings not only provide a platform to showcase your services but also facilitate face-to-face interactions with potential clients and collaborators. Engaging in discussions, attending seminars, and taking part in panels can position you as a knowledgeable leader in your field.

Leveraging online platforms is another essential networking strategy for trade professionals. Social media channels like LinkedIn, Facebook, and Instagram offer unique opportunities to connect with other business owners, industry experts, and potential clients. By regularly sharing valuable content, engaging with followers, and participating in relevant groups, you can increase your visibility and enhance your credibility. Additionally, utilizing online forums and industry-specific websites allows for broader outreach and the chance to contribute to discussions relevant to your trade. This digital presence can foster relationships that may lead to referrals and partnerships.

Developing a targeted networking approach is vital for maximizing your efforts. Rather than attempting to connect with everyone in your field, focus on building relationships with individuals and businesses that align with your goals. Identify key influencers, potential partners, and clients within your niche. Once you have pinpointed these connections, create a personalized outreach strategy that highlights mutual benefits. This approach not only demonstrates your professionalism but also increases the likelihood of forming meaningful and productive relationships.

Follow-up is a critical aspect of effective networking that is often overlooked. After meeting someone at an event or connecting online, it is essential to maintain communication. Sending a personalized follow-up message can serve as a reminder of your discussion and help solidify the relationship. Regularly check in with your contacts, share relevant articles, or invite them to events you are hosting. This consistent engagement will keep you top-of-mind and can lead to valuable referrals and collaborations in the future.

Lastly, consider joining local and national trade associations related to your business. These organizations often provide resources, networking events, and training opportunities that can enhance your skills and expand your network. Being part of such associations gives you access to a community of like-minded professionals who understand the challenges and opportunities within your trade. This environment fosters collaboration and support, allowing you to share experiences and learn from others while building a solid foundation for your brand in the industry.

Collaborating with Other Professionals

Collaborating with other professionals can significantly enhance the visibility and credibility of trade businesses. When trade business owners partner with complementary businesses, they not only expand their network but also tap into new customer bases. For instance, a plumbing company might collaborate with a local construction firm, providing exclusive discounts to their clients while gaining referrals in return. This symbiotic relationship fosters trust among customers, as they are more likely to choose a service recommended by someone they already trust. Thus, identifying the right partners is crucial for successful collaboration.

In addition to building referral networks, collaboration can also enhance branding efforts. When trade professionals align their branding with other reputable businesses, they can elevate their own brand identity. Joint marketing efforts, such as co-hosting events or participating in community projects, can showcase the strengths of each business while reinforcing their commitment to quality and service. Moreover, these collaborations can be highlighted on social media and in marketing materials, creating a cohesive message that resonates with a broader audience. By presenting a united front, trade businesses can reinforce their brand values and attract customers who appreciate collaboration and community engagement.

Referral marketing techniques are particularly effective when combined with professional collaborations. Trade business owners can implement referral programs that incentivize partners to refer clients to one another. For example, offering a commission or a discount for successful referrals can motivate partners to actively promote each other's services. This not only drives new business but also strengthens relationships within the network. Additionally, trade professionals can co-create content, such as blog posts or videos, that highlight their partnership and the benefits it brings to customers, further enhancing the referral marketing strategy.

Networking events and trade shows provide excellent opportunities for collaboration. Attending industry-specific gatherings allows trade business owners to meet potential partners, share ideas, and discuss collaboration opportunities in person. These events can serve as platforms to showcase each other's services, facilitating introductions that may lead to mutually beneficial partnerships. Furthermore, participating in panel discussions or workshops can position trade professionals as thought leaders in their fields, attracting more attention to their brands and fostering new connections.

Lastly, maintaining ongoing communication with partners is essential for successful collaborations. Regular check-ins and updates can help trade business owners assess the effectiveness of their partnerships and make necessary adjustments. Sharing successes and challenges fosters transparency and strengthens relationships, ensuring that both parties benefit from the collaboration. By prioritizing communication and collaboration, trade professionals can create a powerful network that not only enhances their branding and marketing efforts but also contributes to long-term business success.

07

Chapter 7: Measuring Your Brand Success

Key Performance Indicators for Branding

Key Performance Indicators (KPIs) for branding are essential metrics that trade business owners should monitor to assess the effectiveness of their branding efforts. These indicators provide a quantifiable means to evaluate how well a brand resonates with its target audience and supports overall business objectives. By focusing on specific KPIs, trade businesses can make informed decisions to refine their branding strategies and enhance their market presence.

One of the primary KPIs for branding is brand awareness. This metric measures how familiar potential customers are with a brand. Trade business owners can gauge brand awareness through surveys, social media engagement, and website traffic analysis. A higher level of awareness often translates to increased trust and credibility, which are crucial for trade professionals seeking to establish long-term relationships with clients. Tracking changes in brand awareness over time can help identify the effectiveness of marketing campaigns and adjustments made to the brand identity.

Another important KPI is brand perception. This refers to how customers view and feel about a brand, encompassing aspects such as quality, reliability, and value. Trade business owners can assess brand perception through customer feedback, reviews, and social listening tools. Understanding the nuances of how a brand is perceived allows business owners to address any negative sentiments and leverage positive feedback in their marketing efforts. By aligning brand perception with the desired image, trade professionals can create a more compelling brand narrative that attracts and retains clients.

Customer loyalty and retention rates also serve as vital KPIs for branding. These metrics indicate the degree to which customers repeatedly choose a brand over competitors. For trade businesses, high loyalty and retention rates suggest that branding efforts are successful in building relationships and delivering value. Business owners can track these rates through repeat purchase analysis, customer surveys, and loyalty programs. By enhancing customer loyalty through effective branding, trade professionals can benefit from word-of-mouth referrals, which are particularly valuable in the trade sector.

Lastly, the return on investment (ROI) from branding initiatives is a crucial KPI that trade business owners should consider. This metric assesses the financial impact of branding efforts relative to the costs incurred. By analyzing sales growth, customer acquisition costs, and overall profitability, trade professionals can determine the effectiveness of their branding strategies. A positive ROI indicates that branding investments are yielding fruitful results, while a negative ROI may signal the need for strategic reassessment. Monitoring ROI enables trade business owners to allocate resources effectively and focus on initiatives that drive brand success.

Tools for Tracking Brand Metrics

In the competitive landscape of trade businesses, effectively tracking brand metrics is essential for understanding performance and guiding strategic decisions. Various tools are available to help trade professionals gauge their brand's health and reach. These tools can provide insights into customer engagement, brand awareness, and overall market perception, allowing business owners to make informed adjustments to their branding strategies.

One of the primary tools for tracking brand metrics is social media analytics. Platforms like Facebook, Instagram, and LinkedIn offer built-in analytics that provide valuable data on engagement rates, audience demographics, and content performance. By monitoring these metrics, trade business owners can identify which types of content resonate most with their audience and tailor their marketing efforts accordingly. This real-time feedback loop enhances the effectiveness of branding campaigns and helps maintain a strong online presence.

Another valuable resource is customer feedback and survey tools. Services such as SurveyMonkey or Google Forms enable trade professionals to collect direct feedback from customers regarding their brand experience. Understanding customer perceptions and satisfaction levels can illuminate strengths and weaknesses within the brand Identity. Additionally, tools like Net Promoter Score (NPS) can quantify customer loyalty and willingness to refer, providing a clear metric to assess brand health over time.

Website analytics tools, such as Google Analytics, are also crucial for tracking brand metrics. These tools allow business owners to monitor website traffic, user behavior, and conversion rates. Analyzing this data helps in understanding how customers interact with the brand online and which marketing channels drive the most traffic. Insights gained from website analytics can inform branding strategies, improve user experience, and optimize marketing efforts to better align with customer needs.

Lastly, reputation management tools like Brandwatch or Mention can help trade business owners track brand mentions across the web and social media. These platforms provide insights into how the brand is perceived in real-time, allowing businesses to respond proactively to any negative feedback or emerging trends. By monitoring brand sentiment and engagement levels, trade professionals can position themselves effectively within their market and foster a positive brand image that encourages referrals and repeat business.

Adjusting Strategies Based on Feedback

Adjusting strategies based on feedback is a crucial aspect of maintaining relevance and effectiveness in the competitive landscape of trade businesses. Trade business owners must recognize that feedback serves as a powerful tool for growth and improvement. By actively seeking input from customers, employees, and industry peers, business owners can identify areas of strength and weakness in their branding and marketing strategies. This iterative process of adjustment ensures that businesses remain aligned with market demands and customer expectations.

One effective method for gathering feedback is through customer surveys. By designing targeted questions that focus on various aspects of their experience, trade business owners can gain insights into customer satisfaction, brand perception, and service quality. Analyzing the results of these surveys allows businesses to pinpoint specific areas for improvement and to understand which elements of their branding resonate most with their audience. Moreover, maintaining open lines of communication encourages customers to share their thoughts directly, fostering a sense of trust and loyalty.

Trade professionals should also consider utilizing social media and online review platforms to collect feedback. These platforms provide a wealth of information regarding customer opinions and experiences. Monitoring online discussions about their brand can provide real-time insights into how their marketing efforts are perceived. By engaging with customers on these platforms, business owners can demonstrate their commitment to customer satisfaction, address any concerns, and showcase how their brand adapts based on feedback.

Once feedback has been collected and analyzed, the next step is to implement changes effectively. This may involve revising branding elements, adjusting marketing strategies, or enhancing customer service practices. Trade business owners should prioritize feedback that aligns with their long-term goals and values. It is essential to communicate any changes made in response to feedback to customers, as this transparency reinforces their importance in the business's evolution and helps build stronger relationships.

Finally, an ongoing commitment to adjusting strategies based on feedback is vital for sustained success. Trade business owners should establish regular intervals for reviewing customer input and assessing the effectiveness of implemented changes. This proactive approach not only keeps businesses adaptable but also demonstrates to customers that their opinions genuinely matter. By fostering a culture of continuous improvement, trade professionals can enhance their branding, marketing efforts, and ultimately, their overall business performance.

08

Chapter 8: Future Trends in Trade Branding

Emerging Trends in Marketing

Emerging trends in marketing are continually reshaping the landscape for trade business owners. As technology advances and consumer behavior evolves, it becomes imperative for trade professionals to adapt their marketing strategies. One notable trend is the rise of digital marketing, which encompasses social media, content creation, and search engine optimization. Trade businesses that effectively leverage digital channels can enhance their visibility and reach a broader audience. Understanding platforms like LinkedIn, Instagram, and Facebook is crucial as these networks allow for targeted advertising and engagement with potential customers.

Another significant trend is the emphasis on personalization. Today's consumers expect tailored experiences, and trade businesses must learn to cater to these preferences. By utilizing data analytics and customer insights, trade professionals can create personalized marketing campaigns that resonate with their audience. This can include targeted email campaigns, customized offers, and content that addresses specific customer needs. Personalization not only improves customer satisfaction but also enhances brand loyalty, which is vital for long-term success in the competitive trade industry.

Sustainability is also becoming a central theme in marketing strategies. Trade businesses are increasingly recognizing the importance of environmentally friendly practices and how they can be integrated into branding efforts. Consumers are more inclined to support businesses that demonstrate a commitment to sustainability. By showcasing eco-friendly practices, such as using sustainable materials or reducing waste, trade professionals can differentiate their brands and appeal to a growing segment of environmentally conscious customers. This trend not only boosts brand reputation but also aligns with a global push toward sustainable practices in various industries.

Referral marketing continues to be an indispensable tool for trade business owners. With the advent of social media, word-of-mouth has transformed into a powerful digital phenomenon. Trade professionals can harness the influence of satisfied customers by encouraging referrals through incentives or loyalty programs. Creating a referral network not only drives new business but also builds trust, as recommendations from friends or family are often perceived as more credible than traditional advertising. Fostering a community of advocates around a brand can lead to sustained growth and a strong market presence.

Lastly, the integration of artificial intelligence (AI) into marketing strategies is revolutionizing how trade businesses operate. AI can analyze consumer behavior, predict trends, and automate marketing processes, allowing trade professionals to focus on strategic decision-making. Chatbots and virtual assistants are becoming commonplace, providing immediate assistance to customers and enhancing their experience. By adopting AI technologies, trade business owners can optimize their marketing efforts, improve customer engagement, and streamline operations, ensuring they remain competitive in an ever-evolving marketplace.

The Impact of Technology on Branding

The impact of technology on branding is profound and multifaceted, presenting trade business owners with both challenges and opportunities. As digital platforms evolve, so too do the methods by which brands communicate their values, engage with customers, and differentiate themselves from competitors. The shift towards online interactions means that branding strategies must be adaptable and responsive to the changing landscape, requiring business owners to stay informed about the latest technological advancements and their implications for marketing and brand identity.

One of the most significant technological advancements influencing branding is the rise of social media. Platforms like Facebook, Instagram, and LinkedIn have become essential tools for trade professionals seeking to build their brand presence. These channels allow businesses to showcase their work, share customer testimonials, and engage with their audience in real-time. By leveraging social media effectively, trade business owners can create a more personal connection with their customers, enhancing brand loyalty and driving referrals. Understanding the nuances of each platform is crucial, as it enables businesses to tailor their messaging and visual content to resonate with their target audience.

Additionally, the advent of data analytics tools has transformed how trade businesses approach branding. With access to detailed insights about customer behavior, preferences, and engagement, business owners can make informed decisions about their branding strategies. This data-driven approach allows for the customization of marketing efforts, ensuring that brands communicate their messages in ways that are most likely to resonate with specific segments of their audience. The ability to track and analyze campaign performance in real-time also facilitates continuous improvement, enabling businesses to refine their branding tactics based on measurable outcomes.

Moreover, technology has revolutionized the way trade professionals can manage their brand identity across various channels. Content management systems and digital asset management tools allow for a cohesive presentation of branding elements, ensuring consistency across platforms. This is particularly important in establishing credibility and trust with customers. As potential clients increasingly rely on online reviews and recommendations, maintaining a strong and consistent brand identity becomes imperative. Trade business owners must harness technology to streamline their branding efforts, making it easier to maintain quality and coherence in their messaging.

Lastly, emerging technologies, such as artificial intelligence and augmented reality, are paving the way for innovative branding strategies. AI can help personalize customer experiences, allowing businesses to tailor their offerings based on individual preferences and behaviors. Augmented reality can enhance customer engagement by providing interactive experiences that allow clients to visualize products or services in their own environments. Trade business owners who embrace these technologies can set their brands apart in a crowded marketplace, creating memorable experiences that not only attract new customers but also foster loyalty among existing ones. Adapting to these technological advancements is essential for trade professionals aiming to build a resilient and recognizable brand in today's dynamic business environment.

Preparing for Changes in Consumer Behavior

Preparing for changes in consumer behavior is essential for trade business owners looking to maintain a competitive edge in an ever-evolving market. The complexities of consumer preferences, driven by technological advancements and social shifts, necessitate a proactive approach to branding and marketing strategies. Understanding these shifts allows trade professionals to align their offerings with the expectations and demands of their target audience, thereby enhancing customer loyalty and driving growth.

One key aspect of preparing for changes in consumer behavior involves staying informed about industry trends and consumer insights. Trade business owners should leverage market research tools and analytics to gather data on consumer preferences, behaviors, and buying patterns. This information can reveal critical insights into what customers value most, whether it's sustainability, convenience, or price sensitivity. By continuously monitoring these trends, business owners can adapt their branding strategies and marketing initiatives to resonate with the evolving needs of their clientele.

Another effective strategy is to engage with customers through various channels, fostering open lines of communication. Utilizing social media, surveys, and feedback forms enables trade professionals to gain direct insights into consumer sentiments and preferences. This engagement not only helps in understanding the current landscape but also aids in anticipating future changes. By cultivating a community around their brand, trade business owners can create a loyal customer base that feels valued and heard, ultimately guiding their branding efforts to reflect consumer desires accurately.

In addition to understanding consumer tendencies, trade business owners should focus on enhancing their digital presence. As consumers increasingly turn to online platforms for information and purchasing decisions, a robust online identity becomes critical. Investing in a user-friendly website, optimizing for search engines, and maintaining active social media profiles can significantly impact how consumers perceive a brand. The digital landscape also provides opportunities for targeted advertising and personalized marketing, allowing trade professionals to reach potential customers more effectively and efficiently.

Lastly, business owners must be adaptable and willing to pivot their strategies when necessary. The rapid pace of change in consumer behavior can render certain marketing tactics obsolete. Therefore, fostering a culture of innovation within the organization is crucial. Encouraging team members to share ideas and experiment with new approaches can lead to breakthroughs in branding and marketing strategies. By remaining flexible and responsive to consumer feedback, trade business owners can ensure their brand evolves alongside their audience, securing their position in a competitive market.

09

Chapter 9: Case Studies of Successful Trade Brands

Analyzing Effective Branding Strategies

Effective branding strategies are crucial for trade business owners looking to establish a strong presence in their respective markets. Understanding the components of a successful brand can significantly influence customer perception and loyalty. A brand is not just a logo or a catchy slogan; it's the overall experience and value that a business delivers to its clients. Trade business owners must first identify their unique selling propositions (USPs) and core values, as these elements form the foundation upon which a brand is built. By clearly defining what sets their services apart and what they stand for, trade businesses can create a compelling narrative that resonates with their target audience.

Consistency is another vital aspect of effective branding. Trade business owners should ensure that their branding elements—such as logos, color schemes, and messaging—are uniform across all platforms and marketing materials. This consistency helps build recognition and trust among potential clients. When customers encounter a brand that presents itself uniformly, they are more likely to remember it and develop a sense of familiarity. Additionally, maintaining a consistent voice in communications, whether in advertisements, social media, or direct interactions, reinforces the brand identity and enables businesses to cultivate a reliable image in the eyes of their audience.

Engaging storytelling is an effective strategy that trade business owners can leverage to connect with their audience emotionally. By sharing their brand story—how they started, the challenges they faced, and their vision for the future—business owners can foster a deeper connection with clients. This narrative can be woven into marketing campaigns and showcased through various channels, including social media, email newsletters, and website content. Storytelling not only humanizes the brand but also invites customers to become part of that journey, creating a sense of belonging and loyalty that can significantly enhance referral marketing efforts.

Incorporating feedback and adapting to market trends are essential for refining branding strategies. Trade business owners should actively seek customer feedback through surveys, reviews, and social media interactions. This feedback can provide valuable insights into customer preferences and pain points, allowing businesses to adjust their branding and offerings accordingly. Moreover, staying attuned to industry trends and competitor strategies can help identify opportunities for differentiation. A responsive approach to branding not only demonstrates a commitment to customer satisfaction but also positions the business as a proactive and innovative player in the market.

Finally, leveraging referral marketing can amplify the effectiveness of branding strategies. Trade business owners can encourage satisfied clients to share their positive experiences with others, creating a ripple effect that enhances brand visibility. Implementing referral programs that reward clients for bringing in new business can further incentivize this behavior. By integrating referral marketing into their branding strategy, trade businesses can tap into the power of word-of-mouth, which remains one of the most trusted forms of advertising. This synergy between branding and referral marketing can lead to sustainable growth and long-term success in the competitive landscape of trade businesses.

Lessons Learned from Industry Leaders

Industry leaders in the trade sector offer invaluable insights that can significantly influence the branding and marketing strategies of trade business owners. One of the most prominent lessons learned is the importance of a strong brand identity. Industry leaders emphasize that a well-defined brand not only sets a business apart from its competitors but also fosters trust and recognition among consumers. By investing in a cohesive brand identity that reflects the values and mission of the business, trade professionals can build lasting relationships with their customers, leading to increased loyalty and repeat business.

Another critical lesson from industry leaders is the power of targeted marketing. Successful trade businesses understand that generic marketing efforts often fall flat. Instead, they advocate for a focused approach that targets specific customer segments. By identifying the unique needs and preferences of their target audience, trade business owners can tailor their marketing messages and campaigns to resonate with potential clients. This strategic approach not only enhances engagement but also improves conversion rates, as customers are more likely to respond to marketing that speaks directly to their interests.

Referral marketing is a powerful tool that industry leaders frequently highlight. Many successful trade businesses have built their reputation on word-of-mouth referrals, which often stem from satisfied customers. By encouraging existing clients to share their positive experiences and offering incentives for referrals, trade business owners can tap into a cost-effective and impactful marketing strategy. Industry leaders recommend creating a structured referral program that rewards customers for bringing in new business, thereby leveraging the power of personal recommendations to expand their customer base.

Additionally, industry leaders stress the importance of consistent communication with clients. Regular updates about services, promotions, and industry trends help maintain engagement and keep the business top-of-mind for customers. This communication can take various forms, including newsletters, social media updates, and personalized emails. By maintaining an open line of communication, trade business owners not only reinforce their brand identity but also position themselves as industry experts, creating a sense of authority and trust among their audience.

Lastly, adaptability is a key lesson learned from industry leaders. The trade industry is constantly evolving, and successful business owners are those who remain flexible and responsive to changes in the market. Embracing new technologies, trends, and consumer behaviors can provide a competitive edge. Industry leaders encourage trade professionals to continuously evaluate their branding and marketing strategies, ensuring they align with current market demands and customer expectations. By fostering a culture of innovation and adaptability, trade business owners can sustain growth and remain relevant in a dynamic industry landscape.

Applying Case Study Insights to Your Business

Applying case study insights to your business can be a transformative approach for trade professionals seeking to enhance their branding, marketing strategies, and overall business performance. By examining real-life examples of successful trade businesses, owners can identify best practices, innovative strategies, and potential pitfalls. These insights provide a practical framework that can be tailored to fit the unique circumstances of each trade business, allowing owners to implement proven tactics that align with their branding objectives.

One of the most effective ways to leverage case studies is to focus on the branding and identity development of other trade businesses. Analyzing how these companies successfully communicated their unique value propositions can inform your own branding efforts. For instance, consider how a plumbing company utilized customer testimonials and project showcases to build trust and credibility within their community. By adopting similar strategies, such as highlighting your most successful projects or sharing client feedback, you can create a compelling brand identity that resonates with your target audience.

In addition to branding, case studies can reveal effective marketing techniques that resonate within the trade industry. For example, a case study on a successful electrical contractor may spotlight their use of social media advertising to reach local homeowners. By dissecting the strategies that led to increased engagement and conversions, you can adapt these techniques for your own marketing campaigns. Whether it's through targeted ads, email marketing, or content creation, understanding how other businesses have successfully navigated the marketing landscape can inspire fresh ideas and approaches for your own initiatives.

Referral marketing is another critical area where case study insights can be invaluable. Many trade businesses thrive on word-of-mouth referrals, and examining how others have cultivated a referral network can provide actionable strategies. For instance, a landscaping company might have implemented a referral program that rewards clients for bringing in new business. By creating similar incentives and fostering strong relationships with satisfied customers, you can encourage referrals that will expand your client base and enhance your business's reputation.

Ultimately, applying case study insights to your business is about learning from the successes and failures of others in the trade industry. By carefully analyzing their approaches to branding, marketing, and referrals, you can adopt strategies that are proven to work while avoiding common pitfalls. This informed approach not only helps in refining your business practices but also empowers you to forge a path that is both unique and effective in achieving your branding goals.

10

Chapter 10: Building a Sustainable Brand

Incorporating Sustainability into Your Branding

Incorporating sustainability into your branding is not just a trend; it's a strategic approach that resonates with modern consumers. Trade business owners must recognize that today's customers are increasingly concerned about the environmental impact of their purchases. By aligning your brand with sustainable practices, you not only differentiate yourself in a competitive marketplace but also build trust and loyalty with your clientele. This alignment can be achieved through transparent communication of your sustainable practices, be it sourcing materials responsibly, reducing waste, or supporting local communities.

To effectively integrate sustainability into your branding, start by evaluating your current practices. Identify areas where your business can minimize its environmental footprint. This could involve using eco-friendly materials, adopting energy-efficient processes, or implementing recycling programs. Once you have made these changes, document them and communicate them clearly in your marketing materials. Highlighting specific initiatives can position your brand as a leader in sustainability within your niche, attracting customers who prioritize eco-conscious choices.

Your branding strategy should also incorporate storytelling that emphasizes your commitment to sustainability. Share real-life examples of how your business is making a difference, whether through community engagement or innovative eco-friendly solutions. This narrative not only enhances your brand identity but also connects emotionally with consumers. By showcasing your dedication to sustainability, you create a compelling reason for customers to choose your services over competitors who may not prioritize these values.

In addition to consumer-facing branding, consider how sustainability can enhance your referral marketing techniques. Encourage satisfied customers to share their positive experiences not only with your products or services but also with your sustainable practices. This can be a powerful incentive for word-of-mouth marketing, as individuals are often eager to recommend businesses that align with their values. Create referral programs that reward customers for spreading the word about your commitment to sustainability, thereby leveraging their networks to expand your reach.

Finally, regularly assess and refine your sustainability initiatives to ensure they remain relevant and impactful. Engage with your customers to gather feedback on your sustainability efforts and their perceptions of your brand. This ongoing dialogue can help you identify new opportunities for improvement and innovation. By continuously evolving your sustainable practices and integrating them into your branding strategy, you will not only enhance your brand's reputation but also contribute positively to the environment, ensuring long-term success for your trade business.

Engaging with Your Community

Engaging with your community is a crucial aspect of building a strong brand identity as a trade business owner. It involves creating meaningful interactions with local residents, other businesses, and potential clients. By actively participating in your community, you not only enhance your reputation but also establish a network of relationships that can lead to referrals and increased customer loyalty. Understanding the needs and interests of your community will allow you to tailor your services and marketing strategies accordingly, ensuring that your brand resonates with your target audience.

One effective way to engage with your community is through sponsorship and involvement in local events. Whether it's sponsoring a youth sports team, participating in community fairs, or hosting workshops, these activities provide visibility and demonstrate your commitment to the welfare of the community. When people associate your business with positive community contributions, they are more likely to choose your services over competitors. Additionally, these events create opportunities for face-to-face interactions, allowing you to build rapport and trust with potential customers.

Another important aspect of community engagement is leveraging social media platforms to connect with local audiences. By sharing local news, participating in discussions, and highlighting community achievements, you can position your brand as a proactive member of the community. Create content that reflects local culture and interests, and encourage user-generated content by asking followers to share their own experiences with your services. This not only boosts your online presence but also fosters a sense of community around your brand, making it more relatable and approachable.

Incorporating feedback from community members into your business operations can also enhance your engagement. Regularly seek input through surveys or informal conversations to understand their needs and preferences. This approach demonstrates that you value their opinions, and it can provide you with insights that help refine your services and marketing strategies. Moreover, showcasing how you have implemented community suggestions reinforces your commitment to customer satisfaction and strengthens your brand identity.

Finally, establishing partnerships with other local businesses can amplify your community engagement efforts. Collaborate on joint marketing initiatives, cross-promotions, or service packages that benefit both parties. These partnerships not only extend your reach but also foster a sense of unity within the community. By supporting each other, you create a network that encourages word-of-mouth referrals and builds a stronger, more recognizable brand. Engaging with your community in these diverse ways will not only enhance your brand identity but also establish a loyal customer base that will support your trade business for years to come.

Long-Term Brand Management Strategies

Long-term brand management strategies are essential for trade business owners aiming to establish a sustainable competitive advantage in their respective markets. These strategies encompass a range of practices that focus on building and maintaining a strong brand identity over time. Trade professionals must prioritize consistency in their branding efforts, ensuring that all touchpoints—whether online or offline—reflect the core values and mission of the business. This consistency not only fosters brand recognition but also builds trust with clients, setting the foundation for long-lasting relationships.

One of the most effective long-term brand management strategies is the development of a comprehensive brand identity system. This includes creating a visual identity, such as logos and color schemes, as well as defining brand messaging that resonates with the target audience. Trade business owners should invest time in understanding their market and developing a unique value proposition that differentiates them from competitors. A well-defined brand identity helps to establish a recognizable presence in the marketplace, making it easier for customers to identify and engage with the brand.

Another crucial aspect of long-term brand management is the cultivation of customer loyalty. Trade professionals can achieve this by implementing referral marketing techniques that encourage satisfied customers to share their positive experiences with others. By creating referral programs that reward clients for recommendations, businesses can not only enhance their brand visibility but also foster a community of loyal advocates. This word-of-mouth marketing is particularly effective in the trade industry, where trust and reputation play significant roles in customer decision-making.

In addition to fostering customer loyalty, trade business owners must also be attentive to brand evolution. The market landscape is constantly changing, and brands must adapt to remain relevant. This involves monitoring industry trends, customer feedback, and competitive strategies to identify opportunities for growth and innovation. Regularly revisiting and refining the brand's messaging and offerings ensures that the business remains aligned with customer expectations and market demands. Embracing change while staying true to core values is key to sustaining brand integrity over time.

Finally, measuring the effectiveness of branding efforts is an integral part of long-term brand management. Trade business owners should establish metrics to evaluate brand performance, including customer engagement, brand awareness, and overall market share. By analyzing these metrics, businesses can gain insights into the strengths and weaknesses of their branding strategies. This data-driven approach allows for informed decision-making, enabling trade professionals to optimize their branding initiatives for better outcomes. Ultimately, a commitment to continuous improvement will help trade businesses thrive in an ever-evolving marketplace.

www.ingramcontent.com/pod-product-compliance
Lightning Source LLC
Chambersburg PA
CBHW071109240526
45469CB00006BD/2402